Keyboard Classics

**7 well-known pieces for piano
by one of the world's greatest composers**

TABLE OF CONTENTS

D1524489

All selections on the CD are performed by
Kim O'Reilly except "Duet from *Don Giovanni*,"
"Aria from *The Marriage of Figaro*," and
"Theme from *Concerto No. 21*," which are
performed by Chie Nagatani.

ISBN 0-7390-1721-7

Cover photo: © Horst Klemm / Masterfile

Wolfgang Amadeus Mozart

Wolfgang Amadeus Mozart was born in Salzburg, Austria, on January 27, 1756. His first efforts at composition began when he was only four years old. By the time he was six he had composed dozens of remarkable pieces for the keyboard as well as for other instruments, and was performing for emperors and empresses in the courts of Europe.

At eight, he startled the King of England by playing at sight every difficult piece of music put before him, and by improvising during public concerts. At the age of 10, he wrote an oratorio, and at 11, he wrote his first opera. At 13 he was appointed Chapel Master at the court of the Archbishop of Salzburg. At 14, he received an advanced degree in music from the Royal Academy in Mantua, Italy, and was knighted by the Pope. By this time, he had successful operas running for weeks of performance at La Scala, the great opera house in Milan, Italy, and was no longer regarded as a child prodigy, but fully recognized as a great master.

Wolfgang's father, Leopold Mozart, was a famous violinist who held an important position as the assistant conductor of the orchestra of the Archbishop of Salzburg. He was a brilliant musician and an outstanding teacher, and he was quick to recognize the unusual talents of his two remarkable children. Wolfgang's sister, Anna Maria (Nannerl), was almost as gifted as her brother. Leopold virtually gave up his post with the court orchestra to devote his time to developing the talents of his two children, and to arranging concert appearances for them.

During his extensive travels, the young Wolfgang was quick to assimilate the best of what he heard from the greatest musicians he encountered. In London, he studied composition with Johann Christian Bach, a son of the great Johann Sebastian Bach. In Germany, he was impressed and influenced by the musical discipline of the famous Mannheim Orchestra, with its remarkable dynamic contrasts, ranging from the softest *pianissimo* to the loudest *fortissimo.* In Bologna, Italy, he was heard by the great Padre Martini, who became his mentor and instructor and helped him to prepare for his degree.

When he was 26 years old, Mozart married Constanze von Weber, over his father's objections. The course of his married life never ran smooth. Although his career was artistically successful, he was a poor business man and had a difficult time managing his affairs, especially after his father was no longer able to travel with him. Although his music was performed all over Europe, even by amateurs and (to Mozart's delight) by street musicians, Mozart died in poor circumstances. Believing that he had been poisoned, perhaps by a jealous musician, he died on December 5, 1791, and was buried in an unmarked grave.

Mozart's works contain the essence as well as the most perfect of those compositions which are correctly called *classical.* His fame came first as a composer and performer of music for the harpsichord, but the piano began to be perfected, and by the time he was 21, he had selected it for his main instrument. He became the first of the great composers for piano.

Of Wolfgang Amadeus Mozart, Haydn said, "He is the greatest composer I know, personally or by reputation. He has taste, and furthermore he has the greatest possible knowledge of composition."

Mozart would never bow to the common practice of allowing royalty to dictate how music should be composed. When the Emperor heard his opera *The Abduction from the Seraglio,* he said, "It is too beautiful, my dear Mozart, and it has far too many notes." Wolfgang answered, quite confidently, "Just exactly as many notes as are needed, Your Majesty."

Minuet in F Major

Track 1

Duet from *Don Giovanni*

Là ci darem la mano

 Track 2

Aria from *The Marriage of Figaro*

Non Più Andrai

 Track 3

Sonata in C Major

1st Movement

Track 4

ⓒ Begin the trill on the upper note (B).

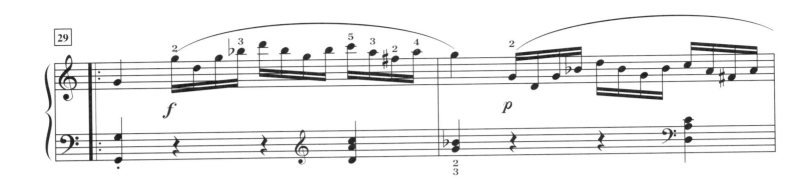

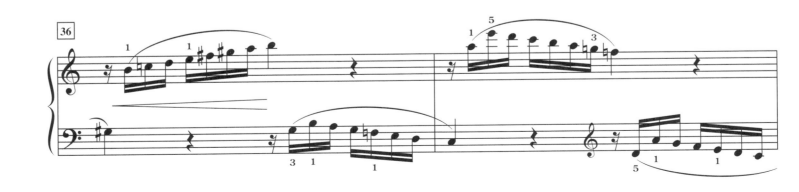

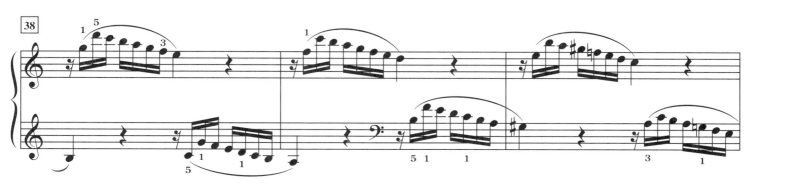

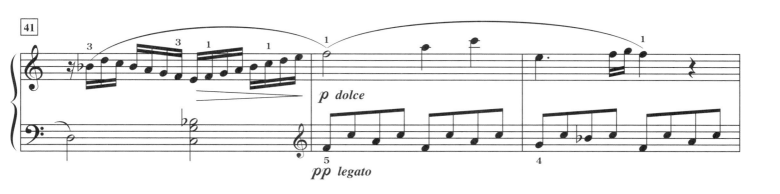

Theme from *Concerto No. 21*

Track 5

(a) Begin the trill on the upper note (F).

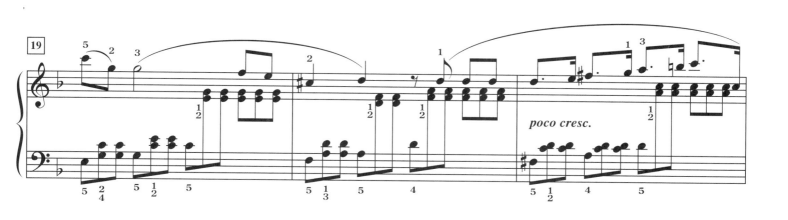

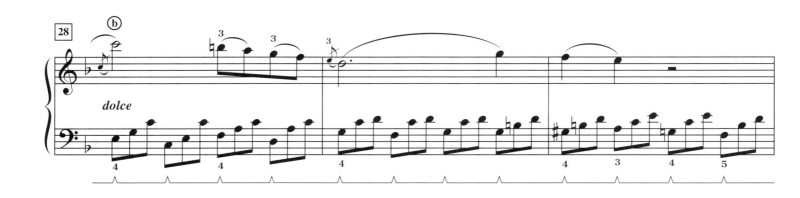

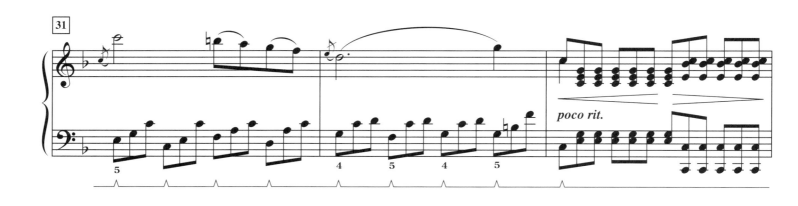

Rondo alla Turca

from *Sonata No. 11 in A Major*

Track 6

ⓐ Play the small notes *very quickly*, with the first one *on the beat*.

ⓑ Play the three small notes *very quickly,* with the first one *on the beat.*

Rondo in D Major

 Track 7

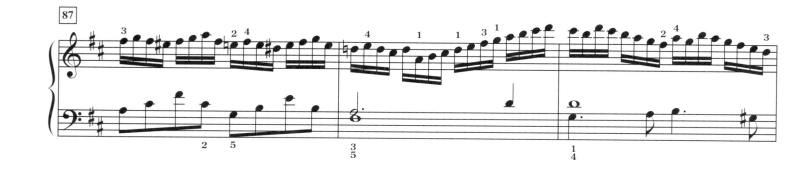

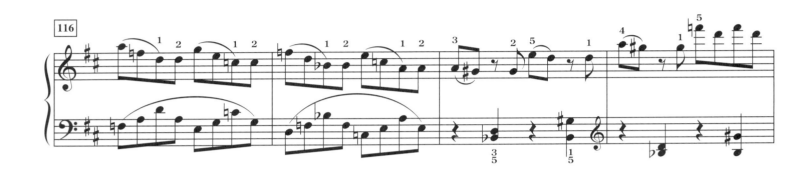